KETO DIET COOKBOOK

FOR BEGINNERS 2019

The Ketogenic Diet Recipes for Busy People on Keto Diet
with 3-week Meal Plan

By Messiah Harris

Legal & Disclaimer

The information contained in this book and its contents is not designed to replace or take the place of any form of medical or professional advice; and is not meant to replace the need for independent medical, financial, legal or other professional advice or services, as may be required. The content and information in this book has been provided for educational and entertainment purposes only.

The content and information contained in this book has been compiled from sources deemed reliable, and it is accurate to the best of the Author's knowledge, information and belief. However, the Author cannot guarantee its accuracy and validity and cannot be held liable for any errors and/or omissions. Further, changes are periodically made to this book as and when needed. Where appropriate and/or necessary, you must consult a professional (including but not limited to your doctor, attorney, financial advisor or such other professional advisor) before using any of the suggested remedies, techniques, or information in this book.

CONTENT

Introduction

Are you struggling to find the best way to lose weight? Well, you can now sit and relax because that came to an end a few seconds ago. I am a living testimony that Keto diet is the ultimate problem solver and is 100% effective.

If you last saw me a year ago, and you see me right now, you would be surprised that I am a totally different person in terms of my size. In that time, I have shed off about half of my weight.

I must say that it's not easy being overweight, or rather weighing way much more than the average person. To make you understand, let's do a flashback of me some years back.

"Harris, you are getting so fat". That was the statement from one of the girls in my class. Me? Fat? No way! "I am not fat", I tried to comfort myself. Honestly speaking, that statement struck me like a sword while deep down I knew it was true. Imagine a situation in school where the boys are trying to get girlfriend you are told you are fat! Moreover, that coming from a lady makes it worse.

I just had to do something immediately that would make me cut my weight. I decided to cut the "fatty" foods that I thought greatly contributed to my weight. I was in college when I noticed that I am becoming "overweight".

Fast-forward three months later I got the shock of my life when I realized that instead of cutting my weight, I had gained two pounds. "How on earth did that happen?" I couldn't help but think that I had made such a joke of myself because the results were the opposite of what I expected. "There has to be a way out of this", I told myself.

In the process of finding a solution, my friend Anthony told me of keto diet. He told me that her mom used that diet and she lost her weight even without having to avoid "fatty" foods like me. That is the moment I made a decision that I will try this diet.

I must say that was the best decision I ever made in regards to my weight. I have managed to cut my weight while enjoying the delicious recipes that are keto. I wished I had earlier met someone to tell me about the amazing keto diet.

With keto diet, there is a wide variety of meals that you can eat. There are snacks, appetizers, poultry, meat and also drinks. You will enjoy the best recipes while you lose weight effortlessly. Who wouldn't want that? I know you want it too. This is the reason why you should go for keto diet and enjoy its full benefits.

This book is the ultimate guide to ketogenic diet. It has all the information that you need to know about keto. The recipes in this book are proven to work. I have cooked every one of them and they are the reason I have cut a lot of weight. Try them today and you will not regret.

Thanks for downloading my book! Enjoy reading!

Chapter 1 The Keto Diet 101

The name "ketogenic" diet comes from the word "ketone." Ketones are small molecules produced in the body and used for fuel when glucose is not available. They are produced in the liver from fat and can then be used throughout the body as a source of energy – they can even be used by the brain!

In order to switch your body from burning glucose for energy to producing ketones, you need to significantly reduce your carbohydrate intake and increase your fat intake so you have energy stores to draw from.

This is the basis of the ketogenic diet – it is a low carb, high fat, moderate protein diet.

To help you understand how the ketogenic diet is different, you need to understand how your body is currently burning energy. If you follow the typical Western diet, you probably eat a lot of grain-based foods, processed carbohydrates, and added sugar. Each of these foods is broken down by the digestive system into their primary components which include glucose.

Glucose is a source of energy that is very easy for the body to burn. When you consume simple carbohydrates (things like processed carbs and sugar), your body breaks them down quickly and the glucose becomes available as a fast-burning source of energy.

When you have more glucose than your body can use in the moment, your body stores the excess in your cells in the form of glycogen. Later, when your body needs more energy, but you haven't eaten recently, it can tap into those glycogen stores to find the energy it needs. If you continue to restrict your carbohydrate intake, your body will burn through those glycogen stores at which point it will need to find another source of energy – that's where ketones come in.

In the absence of glucose, your body starts to burn through your fat stores in a process that produces ketones. Ketones are a highly efficient source of fuel that can be used by the whole body, including your brain.

When your body switches over from burning glucose as energy to burning fat instead, it enters a state of ketosis. The goal of the ketogenic diet is to enter and then maintain this metabolic state in which your body will burn through your stored fat for fuel, helping you lose weight.

The longer you follow the ketogenic diet, the more your body adapts, and you will experience additional benefits. Keep reading to find out what they are.

The Benefits of the Ketogenic Diet

The primary benefit of the ketogenic diet is, of course, weight loss. If you stick to the diet for a while, however, you'll experience a wide range of other benefits. Here is a quick overview of some of the top health benefits associated with the keto diet:

- Fast weight loss without feeling hungry or deprived – fat keeps you feeling full longer than carbohydrates.
- Healthy fat consumption supports cardiovascular health and reduces risk factors such as high blood pressure and high cholesterol.
- The ketogenic diet offers neuroprotective benefits, helping slow the progression of neurodegenerative disease and conditions like Parkinson's and Alzheimer's.
- Could reduce the risk of cancer and may improve the efficacy of cancer treatments – may also reduce the severity of side effects from chemotherapy and radiation treatments.
- Improves microflora balance in the digestive tract for improved skin health – helps to fight chronic acne and other skin conditions.
- May reduce the frequency or severity of seizures in people with seizure disorders like epilepsy – particularly for children with epilepsy.
- Improves symptoms of polycystic ovary syndrome (PCOS) in women and may help treat the condition.
- Increased mental performance – improved concentration and focus.
- Regulates blood sugar levels to help improve or reverse type 2 diabetes – lowers blood sugar levels and helps regulate insulin.
- Improved health markers to prevent chronic diseases.
- May help improve symptoms of mental health issues – may reduce anxiety and depression as well as mood swings.

The benefits you receive from the ketogenic diet depend how well you stick to your macronutrient ratio and how long you follow the diet. There is nothing wrong with following the diet for a few months to meet your goals, but you should consider making the ketogenic diet your long-term eating plan because of all the wonderful health benefits listed above.

Though the ketogenic diet has the potential to provide a great many benefits, it is not the right choice for everyone. If you take medications for diabetes or hypertension, you may want to talk to your doctor before starting the diet.

How Keto Diet Works

For each activity that the body partakes in, there is a considerable amount of energy utilized. This energy comes from a wide range of sources in the body, high on the list being carbohydrates which are quickly converted into glucose –an ever-ready energy. Not only that, the body would also be fueled by fat and protein that is broken down into water soluble particles in the body. However, fat is not as easily digestible into the system as would carbohydrates. Excess fat ends up being stored within the body. For this reason, if you then want to reduce the amount of fat in your body, the idea is to systematically reduce the sugar and carbs in the diet. When the body runs out of ready-to make sugar, it seeks alternate sources of energy.

At this point, ketones come into play. Ketones are created from a combination of three main soluble compounds; acetoacetate, acetone and B-hydroxybutyrate commonly known as BHB. These are produced by the liver in the absence of carbs for energy. All the stored fat and protein begins to be utilized, burnt and converted into ketones for the body to continue functioning well. Ketosis is the state you are in when this happens.

Ketosis can thus be deliberate or a result of starvation or continued fasting, this way ketosis can have positive and negative effects on the body. The safest way to achieve a state of ketosis is the deliberate one, attained through a specially formulated diet which excludes starchy foods and increased protein. In medical scenarios, it has been known since the 1912s that a state where the body is fueled by energy proceeding from fat and protein and no carbs can be extremely beneficial for the body.

This was discovered after testing and observing patients to take a controlled ketogenic diet. After a couple of weeks, patients previously suffering from epileptic episodes showed signs of improvement, experiencing less seizures and better control of their mental faculties. Mayo Clinic's Dr. Russel Wilder then named the "ketogenic diet" and to date it has been prescribed to some patients presenting epilepsy, autism, hypertension and many other ailments because the ketones that fuel the brain enhance brain functionality much better than the energy fueled by carbs.

8 Critical Tips for Entering Ketosis Quickly

Now that you know the benefits of the ketogenic diet and the secret to activating your body's fat-burning switch, all you have to do is take the necessary steps to enter ketosis. If you stick to your macros, you should be able to enter ketosis within 5 to 10 days. Here are some simple tips to expedite the process:

1. Minimize your carbohydrate intake – try to consume no more than 20 grams per day and focus on whole food sources like fresh veggies rather than processed carbohydrates.
2. Maximize your fat intake, focusing on healthy sources like coconut oil, avocado, and other sources of MCTs.
3. Start each day with a brisk 15- to 30-minute walk before breakfast to help burn through your glycogen stores.
4. Make fat the star of every meal and consume moderate amounts of protein with each meal – just try not to go overboard on protein.
5. Try intermittent fasting to encourage your body to enter a state of ketosis more quickly – one easy way is to stop eating at 8pm everyday then have your first meal at noon.
6. Start testing your ketones with a urine test after the first 3 days and make adjustments to your diet as needed.
7. Try taking exogenous ketone supplements to speed up the process of entering a state of ketosis.
8. Track your macros and try to stick within the recommended macronutrient range as much as possible.

As you take the steps above to encourage your body to enter a state of ketosis, know that you may experience some negative side effects along the way. It takes time for your body to adjust to any major change you make to your diet or lifestyle, so be prepared.

Calculating and Tracking Your Macros

The beauty of the ketogenic diet is that it is not a typical crash diet – you don't have to severely restrict your calorie intake. In fact, you don't have to count calories at all!

The key to the ketogenic diet is maintaining the right macronutrient ratio. This simply means that you eat a specific amount of fat, protein, and carbs each day to maintain a specific ratio of macronutrients. As long as you stick to your macros, it doesn't matter all that much how many calories you consume.

But what is the recommended macronutrient ratio for the ketogenic diet?

The idea is to consume most of your daily calories in the form of fat with moderate protein intake and low carb intake. Generally speaking, you want to aim for 70% to 75% of your daily calorie intake to come from fat, 20% to 25% from protein, and no more than 5% from carbohydrates. Some people like to limit their carb intake to 20g or 25g daily, but you have some wiggle room as long as you stick to the right ratio.

What if you want to stick to a certain calorie range?

If your primary goal with the ketogenic diet is to lose weight, you may want to eat at a slight calorie deficit to help boost your results. You can find plenty of free calculators online to help you determine your ideal calorie range, and then you can use that information to determine how many grams of fat, protein, and carbs you can consume to stay within the right ratio.

Here's how to calculate your macros:

1. Take your total daily calorie intake and multiply it by 70% (or 0.70) – this will tell you how many of your daily calories should come from fat.
2. Do the same with 75% to find the upper end of your fat intake range.

3. Take the total number of calories from fat (from Step 1) and divide it by 9 (each gram of fat contains 9 calories).
4. Repeat this with the value from Step 2 – now you know what range you want to stay within for your fat intake.
5. Repeat these four steps with your protein range – you'll need to divide your calories from protein by 4 instead of 9 (each gram of protein contains 4 calories).
6. Repeat with your 5% carbohydrate intake, dividing the total calories from carbs by 4 to determine your daily carb intake in grams.

To show you what this looks like, here is an example using a daily calorie intake of 1,600 calories:

- 1,600 x 70% (0.70) = 1,120 / 9 = 124 grams
- 1,600 x 75% (0.75) = 1,200 / 9 = 133 grams

So, now you can see that your daily macro range for fat should be between 124 and 133 grams. You can do the same calculations for protein, dividing your total calories from protein by 4, and again for carbohydrates. Using these calculations, you can determine your individual macronutrient range based on your daily calorie goals.

By now you should have a thorough understanding of the ketogenic diet and how to make it work for you. All that is left now is to give it a try!

So, turn the page to check out the three weekly meal plans. Each week you'll be preparing easy ketogenic meals in a day-by-day plan designed to help you stick to your macros. Plus, each recipe features no more than 6 main ingredients which means that it is as simple as possible.

If you're ready to get started, just turn the page!

Foods to Eat

Healthy fats

- Saturated (goose fat, tallow, clarified butter / ghee, coconut oil, duck fat, lard, butter, chicken fat)
- Monounsaturated (olive, macadamia and avocado oil)
- Polyunsaturated omega 3s (seafood and fatty fish)

Non-starchy vegetables

- Spinach
- Endive
- Bamboo Shoots
- Asparagus
- Lettuce
- Cucumber
- Kale
- Radishes
- Celery Stalk
- Chives
- Zucchini

Fruits e.g. avocado, berries

Nuts and seeds

Macadamia nuts, pine nuts, walnuts, sunflower seeds, sesame seeds, hemp seeds, pumpkin seeds, pecans, hazelnuts, almonds

Dairy Products

- Cream cheese
- Heavy whipping cream
- Whole milk yogurt (unsweetened)

Beverages

- Water
- Unsweetened herbal tea
- Unsweetened coconut milk
- Decaf coffee
- Unsweetened almond milk
- Unsweetened soy milk
- Unsweetened herbal tea

Protein

Fish: cod, halibut, tuna, salmon, trout, flounder, mackerel, snapper, and catfish.

Meat: Goat, Beef, Lamb, and other wild game

Poultry: Chicken meat, duck meat, and quail meat

Shellfish: Squid, Clams, scallops, lobster, mussels, crab, and oysters,

Whole Eggs

Pork products

Sausage and bacon

Peanut Butter

Dressings

- Balsamic Vinegar
- Ranch
- Blue Cheese
- Apple Cider Vinegar
- Creamy Caesar

Spices

- Oregano
- Black Pepper
- Rosemary
- Basil
- Thyme
- Sea salt

- Cumin
- Parsley

- Sage
- Cayenne Pepper

Foods to Avoid

Processed foods

- Artificial sweeteners: sweeteners containing Aspartame, Equal, Sucralose, Acesulfame, Saccharin, Splenda
- Refined fats / oils e.g. grape seed, corn oil, sunflower
- Alcoholic drinks: beer, cocktails,
- Tropical fruit: papaya, banana, mango, pineapple

Tips for Successful and Happy Ketogenic Lifestyle

The ketogenic lifestyle is enjoyable. You get to enjoy amazingly delicious recipes as you cut your weight. You don't have to eat some nasty tasting foods to achieve your desired weight. Isn't that a win-win? Definitely yes! To make the keto journey happy and more enjoyable, there are some tips that you should follow. Below are the tips that will help you make the keto journey interesting;

Clear carbohydrates from your kitchen

Most people will only stick to the ketogenic diet if they had access to healthy ketogenic foods. This will help you a lot in avoiding falling prey to the carbohydrate concentrated foods in your cabinet. Clean your kitchen from high-carbohydrate foods like pastry, bread, potatoes, soda, rice, and candy. This will help a long way in achieving the ketogenic diet. I must say this helped me a lot in achieving my weight goal

Have ketogenic snacks at hand

Cooking had been a hard thing for me. However, I had made the choice to lose weight and not even having to cook at home would stand on my way. Having to prepare a lot of homemade meals is a big challenge for people as regards the ketogenic diet. There is a solution for you: why not have ketogenic snacks instead whenever you are hungry and you are not at home?

You can buy ketogenic snacks like hard boiled eggs, beef jerky, pre-cooked bacon, pre-made guacamole and so on or you can have them on the go. You can prepare a lot of them and this will not allow you to buy carbohydrate-heavy snacks.

Buy a food scale

This might sound surprising but it is quite crucial. As it has been said, "Drops of water make an ocean." The amount of food you eat matters even to the tiniest form. Buy a food scale to measure your food and make sure you are eating the appropriate size because even the least can make a difference.

For example, 2 extra tablespoons of almond butter turn out to be an additional 200 calories and 6 grams of carbohydrates. It is not necessary you use the food scale till the end of your challenge. It is just for you to get the appropriate measurement then you can eyeball to measure it as you continue.

Exercise frequently

I have mentioned a lot. Exercising allows your body to break down the glycogen it has in store. It also helps you to get fit and healthy. It also helps you in maintaining your muscle mass and strengthens you.

Try intermittent fasting

This is one of the most effective tips that can get you right on track to achieving your fitness goals. It helps you get into ketosis and lose weight. This means that you do not eat anything that contains calories for a given period of time. A study in Harvard has made it known that intermittent fasting manipulates your mitochondria in a way that the ketogenic diet also does and this elongates your lifespan. When you stop taking calories for some time, your body will start breaking down the excess glucose in your body obtained from consuming carbohydrates.

Include coconut oil into your diet

Coconut oil contains fats called medium chain triglycerides which help you to quickly get into ketosis. Unlike other fats, the MCTs get quickly absorbed into the liver where they can be used for energy or they can be converted into ketones.

Some Effects You May Undergo During the Transition

- Headache
- Irritability
- Weakness
- Muscle cramps
- Dizziness
- Nausea
- Vomiting
- Diarrhea
- Poor concentration
- Stomach pain
- Muscle soreness
- Trouble sleeping
- Sugar cravings
- Dehydration

To help reduce the severity of your keto flu symptoms, and to help you get through the transition phase as quickly as possible, make sure you stay hydrated and get plenty of rest. Avoid any strenuous exercise for now and eat some leafy greens and avocado to replace depleted electrolyte stores.

Ketogenic Diet and Weight-Loss

Ketogenic diet enables the breaking down of unwanted fats and stored substances by the body. It is one of the main bodybuilding solutions which helps in lowering fat content in the body while creating muscle. Many of the bodybuilders on keto diet regime set their everyday calorie intake to 20% more than their typical calorie level. The figure is not set but individuals adjust it accordingly. It is not a set figure but a guide and could be adjusted on an individual basis.

It is advised loading up on carbs for a three-day cycle while on keto plan. Eat about 1000 calories of carbs on the third day a couple of hours before exercising. For carb loading, there are two options;

i.   eating what you like
ii.   start with carbs with higher glycemic and then going to the lower ones.

Carb loading is good for intense workout because it enables endurance by enhancing glycogen in the muscles.

For instance, let us say you start off carb-loading on Friday. By Sunday, your muscle tissues will have a substantial amount of glycogen in them. This is the day you ought to exercise. It is optimal to only work out half of the body at this time with weights. Schedule your next exercise routine on Wednesday and be sure to consume 1000 calories worth of carbs prior to your routine. By Wednesday, your glycogen levels will likely be low, but the pre-workout carb load will allow you to work out intensely. This time you will perform exercises targeting the other half of your body.

The next exercise session should be scheduled for Friday at the beginning of the three-day cycle of loading up on carbohydrates. This training session has to be a complete overall body workout with 1-2 sets per workout completed until failure. Make barbell rows, bench presses, military presses, barbell/dumbbell curls, triceps pushdowns, squats, lunges, deadlifts, and reverse curls the focus of your training. The goal of this exercise session is to deplete your glycogen stores within the body completely. Nevertheless, keep cardio to a minimum. Ten-minute warm-ups in advance of each workout is fine, but do not go overboard.

5 Weight Loss Tips During the Keto Journey

1.Keep Your Carbs Very Low

This is the most significant thing while on keto. Maintaining your carbs low helps to get the body into ketosis.

Do not cheat as that will hinder your success and slow the process of your body adapting to ketosis. I once tried cheating during the early stages of my keto journey but then swore never to do it again. "I had made the decision myself and therefore when I cheat, I am only doing to myself", I told myself. Therefore, I advise you to never cheat during your keto journey.

2.Track Your Calories and Macros

This is very important while on keto diet. Carbs are almost everywhere out there and you need to keep track of all that you eat.

3. Watch Your Electrolytes

Electrolytes are of great essence on keto diet as they are removed from the body system.

Ensure that that you take enough potassium, magnesium and sodium to curb excessive hunger, cramps, water retention, headaches and cravings.

4. Be patient

Losing weight does not come overnight. You must consistently work hard over long period of time in order to achieve this goal. Keto diet is a great diet if you want to lose weight. However, you need to know that the weight cannot e lost in a fortnight. It took me more than a month to notice a change in my weight.

5. Enough Sleep and Rest

Stress levels in a person is also a factor in losing you weight. When you are more stressed, the level of cortisol increases which in turn causes weight gain or retention.

Rest is also another factor that is very important. Most people require seven to nine hours of sleep for proper rest of the body each night.

Frequently Asked Questions

Many people I meet ask me various questions about the ketogenic lifestyle. I have analyzed them and came up with the following most frequently asked questions. I answer every question according to my personal experience and interaction with people practicing the keto lifestyle. During my keto journey, I have met people who are practicing the lifestyle. My interaction with these different people has also added to my knowledge of this amazing diet and the many great things it can do.

1.Is Keto Same as Low-Carb?

Low-carb is any diet that has limited carbs. Keto is a type of low-carb meal. However, keto diet is a low-carb diet that is more strict.

2.Can I drink alcohol?

Yes, you can. I love drinking a glass or two of alcohol at least in every two days. Before I started the keto lifestyle, I was worried that alcohol may not be allowed. "Will I manage without even a glass?", I asked myself. However, when I came to learn that I can take a little, I was relieved.

Drinks that have high levels of carbs such as most beers, sweet wines and cocktails are a NO! You are only allowed to take pure liquor and only a maximum of three glasses.

3.Is keto good for weight loss?

Yes. I am a living testimony that keto diet is the best way to lose weight. You will lose your weight as you enjoy amazing recipes.

4.Can pregnant women do the ketogenic diet?

The ketogenic has appeared safe due to the women that have done it and the doctors that have administered it to their patients during pregnancy. I cannot say I am right because there is no scientific research or study that has proved this. So, there is a lack of knowledge concerning this. The ketogenic diet may be very helpful in case of gestational diabetes. It is therefore advised that caution is to be exercised for a ketogenic diet during pregnancy unless there is a benefit you want to achieve while doing it in your own case.

5.Is keto diet good for kids?

It is good to seek a doctor's advice before placing a child on any diet program that is strict. Keto diet has been found to manage cases of epilepsy and autism in children.

6.At what level should my ketones be during ketosis?

Your ketones should be above 0.5mmol/l and this is general.

7.Is the keto diet for vegan/vegetarians?

Yes. Meat is among the staples of ketogenic diet. However, there are a lot of options for any person who is a vegetarian or vegan. I am a meat lover but I also enjoy other nonmeat recipes.

8.Can I develop muscles while doing my ketogenic diet?

Sure! It is even advised to do so but it is not compulsory. You can do this by going to the gym to work out; you can even buy the workout DVD if you do not have the time to go to the gym. Like I said earlier, it is not compulsory.

9. While on Keto, Do I Have to Exercise?

It is not mandatory to exercise while under keto diet. However, if losing weight is your main objective, it's good for you to exercise.

10. How long can I be on the ketogenic diet?

As long as you want! That is why the ketogenic diet is often referred to as a lifestyle. You can do it as long as you desire. It is now more than a year since I started the keto lifestyle and I can tell you that I do not intend to leave it. Not now, not ever! It has become my way of life.

11. How long does it take to be in ketosis?

This is a popular question among those who are just starting the ketogenic diet. I have lost count for the times I have been asked this question. It actually varies from two weeks or more. People with more insulin resistance usually take a longer time before they get to ketosis. Lean and young people usually get to ketosis faster.

Chapter 2 3-week Keto Diet Meal Plans for Beginners

The ketogenic diet is an excellent way to lose weight. While you do not necessarily need to count calories, you do need to stay within the recommended macronutrient ratio in order to enter and maintain a state of ketosis.

Luckily for you, this is easy with the help of three weekly meal plans!

All you have to do is follow the meal plans below. Each day you'll be enjoying quick and easy keto meals for breakfast, lunch, and dinner along with tasty snacks and smoothies. Feel free to enjoy these snacks and smoothies between meals or for dessert – you can customize the meal plan to suit your preferences!

Each recipe used in these meal plans features 6 or fewer main ingredients – that makes them incredibly easy to prepare and it won't bust your grocery budget! Do your best to follow the meal plans because they are designed to keep you within your macronutrient range, so you can maximize your benefits with the ketogenic diet. If you need an additional snack, make sure it is a healthy fat-heavy snack like sliced avocado or sugar-free full-fat Greek yogurt.

So, take a quick look at these meal plans then look for the recipes in the next chapter and weekly shopping lists in the back of the book. Good luck!

Week 1 Meal Plan (Days 1 – 7)

Day	Breakfast	Lunch	Dinner	Snacks	Macros*
1	Ham and Cheddar Omelet with 3 Oz. Deli Ham	Balsamic Spinach Salad with Avocado	Broccoli Salmon Casserole	Almond Green Smoothie	**Calories**: 1730 **Fat**: 130g **Protein**: 110g **Net Carbs**: 21.5g
2	Cream Cheese Pancakes with 4 Slices Bacon	Balsamic Spinach Salad with Avocado and 6 oz. Deli Ham	Leftover Broccoli Salmon Casserole	Chocolate Almond Fat Bomb	**Calories**: 1700 **Fat**: 133.5g **Protein**: 100.5g **Net Carbs**: 17g
3	Leftover Cream Cheese Pancakes with 1 Cup Avocado	Chopped Tuna Salad with 1 Cup Avocado	Steak and Pepper Kebabs	2 Servings Classic Deviled Eggs	**Calories**: 1665 **Fat**: 127g **Protein**: 101.5g **Net Carbs**: 17.5g
4	Fried Eggs in Bell Peppers with 6 Slices Bacon	Leftover Balsamic Spinach Salad with Avocado and 3 Oz. Deli Ham	Leftover Broccoli Salmon Casserole	Chocolate Almond Fat Bomb	**Calories**: 1635 **Fat**: 127g **Protein**: 100g **Net Carbs**: 18g
5	Leftover Cream Cheese Pancakes with 1 Cup Avocado	Leftover Chopped Salad with Tuna and 1 Cup Avocado	Seared Lamb Chops	Cocoa Avocado Smoothie	**Calories**: 1690 **Fat**: 127g **Protein**: 102g **Net Carbs**: 18.5g
6	Leftover Fried Eggs in Bell Peppers with 4 Slices Bacon	Mexican Chicken Soup	Leftover Steak and Pepper Kebabs	Chocolate Almond Fat Bomb and 1 Cup Avocado	**Calories**: 1775 **Fat**: 136.5g **Protein**: 104.5g **Net Carbs**: 20.5g

| 7 | Creamy Coconut Porridge and 6 Slices Bacon | Leftover Mexican Chicken Soup | Leftover Seared Lamb Chops | 2 Servings Classic Deviled Eggs | **Calories**: 1710
Fat: 132g
Protein: 110g
Net Carbs: 15g |

* The daily calorie range for this meal plan is 1,600 to 1,800 calories

Week 1 Shopping List

Eggs, Meat, and Seafood

- Bacon – 20 slices
- Beef, sirloin steak – 12 ounces
- Chicken, boneless thighs – ½ pound
- Eggs – 26 large
- Ham, deli – 12 ounces
- Ham, diced – ½ cup
- Lamb chops, bone-in – 4 chops
- Salmon, Alaskan – 3 (6-ounce) cans
- Tuna, canned in water – 2 (5-ounce) cans

Dairy Products

- Butter – 2 tablespoons
- Cheddar cheese, shredded – 1 ¾ cups
- Cream cheese – ½ (8-ounce) package
- Heavy cream – 1 cup plus 2 tablespoons
- Mayonnaise – ½ cup

Refrigerated and Frozen Foods

- Almond milk, unsweetened – 2 cups
- Yogurt, full-fat Greek, plain – ½ cup

Fresh Fruits and Vegetables

- Avocado – 1 small, 6 medium
- Beans, green – 1 ½ cups
- Bell pepper, red – 2 small, 1 medium
- Broccoli – 1 pound
- Celery – 1 small stalk
- Cucumber, seedless – 1 small
- Garlic – 1 head
- Lemon – 2
- Onion, red – 1 small
- Onion, yellow – 1 small
- Romaine lettuce – 3 cups
- Spinach – 6 cups
- Tomatoes – 1 medium
- Tomatoes, cherry – ½ cup

Dried Goods and Pantry Staples

- Almonds – 8 whole
- Almond butter – ½ cup plus ½ tablespoon
- Almond flour – ½ cup
- Balsamic vinegar
- Broth, chicken – 1 cup
- Cocoa powder, unsweetened
- Coconut flour – 3 tablespoons
- Coconut milk, canned – ¼ cup
- Coconut oil
- Dijon mustard
- Ground psyllium husk
- Liquid stevia extract
- Olive oil
- Paprika
- Pepper
- Salt
- Whey protein powder, chocolate – 1 scoop

Week 2 Meal Plan (Days 8 - 14)

Day	Breakfast	Lunch	Dinner	Snacks	Macros*
8	Bacon Egg Cups with 1 Cup Avocado	Cheesy Cauliflower Soup	Smothered Pork Chops	Almond Butter Protein Shake and Cinnamon Spiced Almonds	**Calories**: 1780 **Fat**: 135.5g **Protein**: 110g **Net Carbs**: 20g
9	Leftover Bacon Egg Cups with 4 Slices Bacon	Bacon Arugula Salad with Mushrooms and Avocado Spinach Smoothie	Herb-Roasted Chicken	Pumpkin Pie Protein Shake	**Calories**: 1710 **Fat**: 126g **Protein**: 116.5g **Net Carbs**: 20g
10	Denver-Style Omelet	Leftover Cheesy Cauliflower Soup	Leftover Herb-Roasted Chicken	Baked Sesame Chia Crackers and Cocoa Almond Smoothie	**Calories**: 1665 **Fat**: 125.5g **Protein**: 108g **Net Carbs**: 22.5g
11	Eggs Baked in Avocado Boats with 4 Slices Bacon	Leftover Cheesy Cauliflower Soup with 6 Slices Bacon	Leftover Smothered Pork Chops	Baked Sesame Chia Crackers and Almond Green Smoothie	**Calories**: 1680 **Fat**: 127.5g **Protein**: 106.5g **Net Carbs**: 22g
12	Leftover Eggs Baked in Avocado Boats with 2 Slices Bacon	Leftover Bacon Arugula Salad with Mushrooms and 4 Slices Bacon	Cheese-Stuffed Burgers	Lemon Avocado Smoothie and Macadamia Nut Fat Bomb	**Calories**: 1690 **Fat**: 128.5g **Protein**: 108.5g **Net Carbs**: 15.5g
13	Three Cheese Omelet	Greek-Style Salad with Feta and 6 Ounces Deli Ham	Leftover Herb-Roasted Chicken	Macadamia Nut Fat Bomb	**Calories**: 1710 **Fat**: 130g **Protein**: 104.5g **Net Carbs**: 16g

| 14 | Spinach Breakfast Bowl with 4 Slices Bacon | Leftover Greek-Style Salad with Feta | Leftover Cheese-Stuffed Burgers | Strawberry Cheesecake Smoothie and Macadamia Nut Fat Bomb | **Calories**: 1690 **Fat**: 129g **Protein**: 112g **Net Carbs**: 16.5g |

* The daily calorie range for this meal plan is 1,600 to 1,800 calories

Week 2 Shopping List

Eggs, Meat, and Seafood

- Bacon – 41 slices
- Beef, ground (80% lean) – 12 ounces
- Chicken, bone-in thighs – 8 thighs
- Eggs – 22 large
- Ham, deli – 6 ounces
- Ham, diced – ¼ cup
- Pork, boneless loin chops – 12 ounces

Dairy Products

- Butter – 1 tablespoon
- Cheddar cheese, shredded – 2 ¾ cups
- Cream cheese – 2 tablespoons
- Feta cheese, crumbled – 1.5 ounces
- Heavy cream – 1 ¼ cups
- Parmesan cheese, grated – 2 tablespoons
- Sour cream – ¼ cup
- Swiss cheese, shredded – 2 tablespoons

Refrigerated and Frozen Foods

- Almond milk, unsweetened – 6 cups
- Yogurt, full-fat Greek, plain – ½ cup

Fresh Fruits and Vegetables

- Arugula, baby – 4 cups
- Avocado – 4 medium
- Beans, green – 1 ½ cups
- Bell pepper, green – 1 small
- Cauliflower – 2 small heads
- Celery – 2 small stalks
- Chives – 1 bunch
- Cucumber, seedless – 1 small
- Garlic – 1 head
- Lemon – 1
- Lettuce, Boston – 1 head
- Lettuce, romaine – 3 cups
- Mushrooms – 3 cups
- Onion, yellow – 1 small
- Raspberries – ¼ cup
- Shallot – 1 small
- Spinach – 6 cups

Dried Goods and Pantry Staples

- Almonds – 1 cup
- Almond butter – ½ cup plus 1 tablespoon
- Almond flour – 1 cup
- Broth, chicken – 2 ½ cups
- Chia seeds – 1 tablespoon
- Cocoa powder, unsweetened
- Coconut flour – 2 tablespoons
- Coconut milk, canned – ½ cup
- Coconut oil
- Dried herbs
- Garlic powder
- Ground cinnamon
- Kalamata olives – ½ cup
- Liquid stevia extract
- Macadamia nuts – 8 whole
- Onion powder
- Olive oil
- Pepper
- Pumpkin pie spice
- Pumpkin puree – 2 tablespoons
- Red wine vinegar
- Salt
- Sesame seeds – ¼ cup
- Vanilla extract
- Whey protein powder, chocolate – 1 scoop
- Whey protein powder, vanilla – 3 scoops

Week 3 Meal Plan (Days 15 - 21)				
Day	**Breakfast**	**Lunch**	**Dinner**	**Snacks**	**Macros***
15	One Pan Eggs and Peppers with 6 Ounces Deli Ham	Cucumber Avocado Soup with 6 Slices Bacon	Grilled Pesto Salmon	Vanilla Chai Smoothie and Sesame Seed Fat Bomb	**Calories**: 1770 **Fat**: 132.5g **Protein**: 110.5g **Net Carbs**: 22g
16	Leftover One Pan Eggs and Peppers with 1 Cup Avocado	Spinach Salad with Bacon Dressing and 4 Slices Bacon	Leftover Grilled Pesto Salmon	Lemon Avocado Smoothie and Sesame Seed Fat Bomb	**Calories**: 1765 **Fat**: 130.5g **Protein**: 112.5g **Net Carbs**: 24.5g
17	Chocolate Protein Pancakes with 2 Slices Bacon	Leftover Cucumber Avocado Soup with 6 Slices Bacon	Rosemary Pork Tenderloin	Cocoa Almond Smoothie with Sesame Seed Fat Bomb	**Calories**: 1760 **Fat**: 136g **Protein**: 114.5g **Net Carbs**: 21.5g
18	Leftover One Pan Eggs and Peppers with 6 Slices Bacon	Leftover Cucumber Avocado Soup with 4 Ounces Deli Ham	Curry Chicken and Broccoli	Pumpkin Pie Protein Shake and Sesame Seed Fat Bomb	**Calories**: 1770 **Fat**: 132g **Protein**: 116g **Net Carbs**: 21.5g
19	Leftover One Pan Eggs and Peppers with 6 Slices Bacon	Leftover Spinach Salad with Bacon Dressing and 1 Cup Avocado	Leftover Rosemary Pork Tenderloin	Sesame Seed Fat Bomb and 2 Ounces Deli Ham	**Calories**: 1750 **Fat**: 133.5g **Protein**: 105.5g **Net Carbs**:23.5g
20	Leftover Chocolate Protein Pancakes	Chopped Cobb Salad with Avocado and 3 Oz. Deli Ham	Leftover Curry Chicken and Broccoli	Coconut Chia Pudding	**Calories**: 1735 **Fat**: 134g **Protein**: 103g **Net Carbs**: 21g

| 21 | Bacon Cheddar Chive Omelet | Leftover Chopped Cobb Salad with ½ Cup Avocado | Leftover Rosemary Pork Tenderloin | Raspberry Coconut Smoothie and 4 Slices Bacon | **Calories**: 1705
Fat: 125.5g
Protein: 110.5g
Net Carbs: 23.5g |

* The daily calorie range for this meal plan is 1,600 to 1,800 calories

Week 3 Shopping List

Eggs, Meat, and Seafood

- Bacon – 40 slices
- Chicken breast, cooked – 1 cup
- Chicken thighs, boneless – 1 ½ pounds
- Eggs – 21 large
- Ham, deli – 17 ounces
- Pork tenderloin, boneless – 1 ¼ pounds
- Salmon, boneless – 2 (6-ounce) fillets

Dairy Products

- Butter – 1 tablespoon
- Blue cheese crumbles – 1 ounce
- Cheddar cheese, shredded – ¼ cup
- Heavy cream – ¼ cup

Refrigerated and Frozen Foods

- Almond milk, unsweetened – 4 cups

Fresh Fruits and Vegetables

- Asparagus – 16 spears
- Avocado – 2 small, 2 medium

- Bell pepper, green – 1 small
- Bell pepper, red – 1 small
- Broccoli – 5 cups
- Celery – 1 small stalk
- Chives – 1 bunch
- Cilantro – 1 bunch
- Cucumber, seedless – 1 medium
- Garlic – 1 head
- Lemon – 2
- Raspberries – 4 whole
- Romaine lettuce – 4 cups
- Rosemary – 1 bunch
- Spinach – 5 cups
- Tomatoes, cherry – ½ cup

Dried Goods and Pantry Staples

- Almond butter – ½ cup
- Almond flour – 2 tablespoons
- Apple cider vinegar
- Chia seeds – ¼ cup
- Cocoa powder, unsweetened
- Coconut extract
- Coconut milk, canned – 3 cups
- Coconut oil
- Curry powder
- Dijon mustard
- Garlic powder
- Ground cinnamon
- Ground cloves
- Ground cumin
- Ground ginger
- Honey
- Liquid stevia extract
- Olive oil
- Pepper
- Pesto – 2 tablespoons
- Pumpkin pie spice
- Pumpkin puree – 2 tablespoons
- Salt
- Sesame seeds, toasted – ¼ cup
- Vanilla extract
- Whey protein powder, chocolate – 1 scoop
- Whey protein powder, vanilla – 2 scoops

Index

A

B

C

Chapter 3 Delicious Keto Recipes

Now that you've seen the three weekly meal plans you'll be following, it's time to take a look at the recipes! Remember, each of these recipes is made with just 6 main ingredients or less to ensure that they are quick and easy to prepare.

You'll notice that there are more recipes included here than are used in the meal plans. Consider them a bonus! Use these extra recipes to create meal plans of your own or swap out one of the recipes from the meal plans for something you prefer.

In the end, what really matters is that you stick to your macros so, however, you can get yourself to do it, call it a win!

Ham and Cheddar Omelet

Servings: 1

Ingredients:

- 3 large eggs
- 2 tablespoons heavy cream
- Salt and pepper
- 1 teaspoon olive oil
- ½ cup diced ham
- ¼ cup shredded cheddar cheese

Instructions:

1. Beat the eggs together with the heavy cream, salt, and pepper then set aside.
2. Heat the oil in a small skillet over medium-high heat.
3. Pour in the egg mixture and let it cook for 1 minute then lift the edges to spread the uncooked egg.
4. Keep cooking until the egg is almost set then sprinkle with cheese and ham.
5. Fold the omelet over then cook until the eggs are set.
6. Slide the omelet onto a plate and garnish with fresh chopped chives to serve.

Nutrition: 580 calories, 46g fat, 38g protein, 5g carbs, 1g fiber, 4g net carbs

Cream Cheese Pancakes

Servings: 3

Ingredients:

- ½ cup almond flour
- ½ (8-ounce) package cream cheese, softened
- 4 large eggs
- 1 tablespoon coconut oil or butter

Instructions:

1. Whisk together the almond flour, cream cheese, and eggs until smooth and well combined.
2. Heat the oil in a large skillet over medium heat.
3. Pour in the batter, using about 3 tablespoons per pancake.
4. Cook until bubbles form in the surface of the batter and the underside is browned.
5. Carefully flip the pancakes and cook until browned underneath.
6. Slide the pancakes onto a plate and repeat with the remaining batter.
7. Serve with sugar-free maple syrup, if desired.

Nutrition: 280 calories, 25g fat, 13g protein, 4g carbs, 1.5g fiber, 2.5g net carbs

Fried Eggs in Bell Peppers

Servings: 2

Ingredients:

- 1 teaspoon olive oil
- 1 medium red bell pepper, cored
- 6 large eggs
- Salt and pepper

Instructions:

1. Heat the oil in a large skillet over medium heat.
2. Slice the bell pepper into rings and place the rings in the skillet.
3. Fry for 2 minutes then flip the rings and crack an egg into the middle of each.
4. Season with salt and pepper then fry until the egg is done to your liking.

Nutrition: 255 calories, 17.5g fat, 19.5g protein, 6g carbs, 1g fiber, 5g net carbs

Bacon Egg Cups

Servings: 4

Ingredients:

- 12 slices uncooked bacon
- 10 large eggs
- ¼ cup sour cream
- ¾ teaspoon garlic powder
- ¼ teaspoon onion powder
- 1 cup shredded cheddar cheese

Instructions:

1. Preheat the oven to 375°F and grease a muffin pan with cooking spray.
2. Cook the bacon in a large skillet until slightly browned but still pliable then remove to paper towels to drain.
3. Whisk together the eggs, sour cream, garlic powder, and onion powder.
4. Stir in the cheese then season with salt and pepper.
5. Line each of the muffin cups with a slice of bacon then spoon in the egg mixture.
6. Bake for 20 minutes until the eggs are set then cool 5 minutes before serving.

Nutrition: 480 calories, 36.5g fat, 34g protein, 3g carbs, 0g fiber, 3g net carbs

Creamy Coconut Porridge

Servings: 1

Ingredients:

- ¼ cup canned coconut milk
- 1 tablespoon coconut oil
- 1 tablespoon coconut flour
- 1 large egg
- Pinch ground psyllium husk
- Pinch salt

Instructions:

1. Whisk together all of the ingredients in a small saucepan.
2. Cook over low heat, stirring constantly until it starts to steam.
3. Keep cooking until thickened to your liking then spoon into a bowl.
4. Top with heavy cream or coconut milk to serve.

Nutrition: 390 calories, 35g fat, 10g protein, 12g carbs, 6.5g fiber, 5.5g net carbs

Denver-Style Omelet

Servings: 1

Ingredients:

- 3 large eggs
- 2 tablespoons heavy cream
- Salt and pepper
- 1 teaspoon olive oil, divided
- ¼ cup diced yellow onion
- ¼ cup diced green pepper
- ¼ cup diced ham
- ¼ cup shredded cheddar cheese

Instructions:

1. Beat the eggs together with the heavy cream, salt, and pepper then set aside.
2. Heat ½ teaspoon of oil in a small skillet over medium-high heat.
3. Add the peppers and onions and sauté for 3 to 4 minutes until tender.
4. Spoon the veggies into a bowl and reheat the skillet with the remaining oil.
5. Pour in the egg mixture and let it cook for 1 minute then lift the edges to spread the uncooked egg.
6. Keep cooking until the egg is almost set then sprinkle half of it with the cooked veggies along with the ham and cheese.
7. Fold the omelet over then cook until the eggs are set.
8. Slide the omelet onto a plate and garnish with fresh chopped chives to serve.

Nutrition: 545 calories, 43g fat, 33g protein, 7.5g carbs, 1.5g fiber, 6g net carbs

Brussels Sprouts Hash

Servings: 4

Ingredients:

- 6 slices bacon, chopped coarsely
- 1 pound brussels sprouts, quartered
- 1 small yellow onion, chopped
- Salt and pepper
- 2 tablespoons water
- 4 large eggs

Instructions:

1. Cook the bacon in a large skillet until crisp then drain on paper towels.
2. Reheat the skillet with the bacon grease and add the brussels sprouts and onion, stirring to coat with bacon fat.
3. Cook for 4 to 5 minutes until the onions soften then season with salt and pepper.
4. Add the water then cover the skillet and steam the brussels sprouts until tender, about 5 minutes.
5. Spread the mixture evenly in the pan then make four depressions with a wooden spoon.
6. Crack an egg into each one then season with salt and pepper.
7. Cover and cook until the eggs are done to your liking then serve hot.

Nutrition: 205 calories, 11g fat, 15.5g protein, 12.5g carbs, 4.5g fiber, 8g net carbs

Cheesy Ham Egg Cups

Servings: 4

Ingredients:

- 12 slices smoked ham
- 1 cup shredded cheddar cheese
- 12 large eggs
- Salt and pepper

Instructions:

1. Preheat the oven to 375°F and grease a muffin pan with cooking spray.
2. Line each cup with a piece of ham.
3. Sprinkle in a little cheese then crack an egg into each cup.
4. Season with salt and pepper then bake 12 to 15 minutes until the eggs are cooked to your liking.

Nutrition: 465 calories, 31.5g fat, 40g protein, 5g carbs, 1g fiber, 4g net carbs

Bacon and Egg Roll-Ups

Servings: 6

Ingredients:

- 6 large eggs
- 2 tablespoons heavy cream
- Salt and pepper
- 1 tablespoon coconut oil
- 18 slices uncooked bacon
- 1 ½ cups shredded cheddar cheese

Instructions:

1. Whisk together the eggs, heavy cream, salt, and pepper.
2. Heat the coconut oil in a large skillet over medium heat then pour in the egg mixture.
3. Cook for 3 minutes, stirring often, until scrambled and done to your liking.
4. Lay out three pieces of bacon on a cutting board.
5. Sprinkle some of the cheese along the bottom third then add a spoonful of scrambled eggs.
6. Roll the bacon up around the filling and repeat with the remaining ingredients.
7. Reheat the skillet and add the roll-ups.
8. Cook for 1 to 2 minutes on each side until the bacon is crisp. Serve hot.

Nutrition: 375 calories, 30.5g fat, 24g protein, 1.5g carbs, 0g fiber, 1.5g net carbs

Three Cheese Omelet

Servings: 1

Ingredients:

- 3 large eggs
- 2 tablespoons heavy cream
- Salt and pepper
- 1 teaspoon olive oil
- 2 tablespoons shredded cheddar cheese
- 2 tablespoons shredded Swiss cheese
- 2 tablespoons grated parmesan cheese

Instructions:

1. Beat the eggs together with the heavy cream, salt, and pepper then set aside.
2. Heat the oil in a small skillet over medium-high heat.
3. Pour in the egg mixture and let it cook for 1 minute then lift the edges to spread the uncooked egg.
4. Keep cooking until the egg is almost set then sprinkle with the cheeses.
5. Fold the omelet over then cook until the eggs are set.
6. Slide the omelet onto a plate and garnish with fresh chopped chives to serve.

Nutrition: 615 calories, 48g fat, 39g protein, 3g carbs, 0g fiber, 3g net carbs

Eggs Baked in Avocado Boats

Servings: 2

Ingredients:

- 1 medium avocado
- 2 large eggs
- Salt and pepper
- 1 teaspoon fresh chopped chives

Instructions:

1. Preheat the oven to 350°F.
2. Cut the avocado in half and scoop some of the flesh out of each half.
3. Place the avocado halves in a baking dish and spray with cooking spray.
4. Crack an egg into each half and season with salt and pepper.
5. Bake for 20 minutes until the eggs are done to your liking then garnish with fresh chopped chives to serve.

Nutrition: 275 calories, 24.5g fat, 8g protein, 9g carbs, 7g fiber, 2g net carbs

Spinach Breakfast Bowl

Servings: 1

Ingredients:

- 2 slices bacon, chopped
- 3 cups fresh baby spinach
- Salt and pepper
- 1 tablespoon butter
- 2 large eggs

Instructions:

1. Cook the bacon in a large skillet over medium-high heat until crisp.
2. Drain the bacon on paper towel then reheat the skillet with the bacon grease.
3. Add the spinach then season with salt and pepper.
4. Cook for 2 to 3 minutes, stirring often, until wilted then place in a bowl.
5. Reheat the skillet with the butter and wait until it is hot.
6. Crack the eggs into the skillet and season with salt and pepper.
7. Cook until the eggs are done to your liking then serve over the spinach topped with crumbled bacon.

Nutrition: 370 calories, 30g fat, 22g protein, 4.5g carbs, 2g fiber, 2.5g net carbs

One-Pan Eggs and Peppers

Servings: 4

Ingredients:

- 10 large eggs
- 2 tablespoons heavy cream
- Salt and pepper
- 1 small red pepper, cored and chopped
- 1 small green pepper, cored and chopped

Instructions:

1. Preheat the oven to 350°F and grease a 9x13-inch glass baking dish.
2. Whisk the eggs and heavy cream in a bowl with the salt and pepper until frothy.
3. Add the peppers and stir well.
4. Pour the mixture into the baking sheet and spread it evenly.
5. Bake for 12 to 15 minutes until the egg is firm and cooked through.
6. Cool for 5 minutes then cut into pieces to serve.

Nutrition: 220 calories, 15g fat, 16g protein, 4.5g carbs, 1g fiber, 3.5g net carbs

Chocolate Protein Pancakes

Servings: 2

Ingredients:

- ½ cup canned coconut milk
- 2 tablespoons coconut oil
- 4 large eggs
- 1 scoop chocolate whey protein powder
- 2 tablespoons unsweetened cocoa powder
- Liquid stevia, to taste

Instructions:

1. Place the coconut milk, coconut oil, and eggs in a blender.
2. Pulse several times then add the protein powder and cocoa powder.
3. Blend the mixture until smooth then sweeten with liquid stevia to taste and blend smooth once more.
4. Heat a large nonstick skillet over medium heat.
5. Spoon the batter into the skillet, using about ¼ cup per pancake.
6. Cook until the underside of each pancake is browned then flip and cook until browned underneath.
7. Slide the pancakes onto a plate and repeat with the remaining batter.

Nutrition: 440 calories, 39g fat, 20g protein, 8g carbs, 3g fiber, 5g net carbs

Bacon Cheddar Chive Omelet

Servings: 1

Ingredients:

- 3 large eggs
- 2 tablespoons heavy cream
- Salt and pepper
- 2 slices bacon, chopped
- ¼ cup shredded cheddar cheese
- 1 tablespoon fresh chopped chives

Instructions:

1. Beat the eggs together with the heavy cream, salt, and pepper then set aside.
2. Cook the bacon in a small skillet over medium-high heat until crisp.
3. Spoon the bacon off into a bowl and reheat the skillet with the bacon grease.
4. Pour in the egg mixture and let it cook for 1 minute then lift the edges to spread the uncooked egg.
5. Keep cooking until the egg is almost set then sprinkle with the cooked bacon along with the cheddar cheese and chives.
6. Fold the omelet over then cook until the eggs are set.
7. Slide the omelet onto a plate and serve hot.

Nutrition: 535 calories, 43g fat, 34g protein, 3g carbs, 0g fiber, 3g net carbs

Lunch Recipes

Balsamic Spinach Salad with Avocado

Servings: 3

Ingredients:

- ¼ cup olive oil
- 2 tablespoons balsamic vinegar
- 1 teaspoon Dijon mustard
- 5 cups fresh baby spinach
- 1 medium avocado, sliced thin

Instructions:

1. Whisk together the olive oil, balsamic vinegar, and Dijon mustard in a salad bowl.
2. Toss with the spinach then divide between two salad plates.
3. Top each salad with sliced avocado to serve.

Nutrition: 295 calories, 30g fat, 3g protein, 8g carbs, 6g fiber, 2g net carbs

Cheesy Cauliflower Soup

Servings: 3

Ingredients:

- 2 cups chicken broth
- 1 small head cauliflower, chopped
- 1 clove minced garlic
- ½ cup heavy cream
- ½ cup shredded cheddar cheese
- Salt and pepper

Instructions:

1. Warm the chicken broth in a medium saucepan over medium heat.
2. Add the cauliflower and garlic then bring to a boil.
3. Reduce heat and simmer for 15 minutes until the cauliflower is tender
4. Stir in the cream and cheese then season with salt and pepper.
5. Blend or use an immersion blender to puree and serve hot.

Nutrition: 195 calories, 15g fat, 10g protein, 6.5g carbs, 2g fiber, 4.5g net carbs

Chopped Salad with Tuna

Servings: 2

Ingredients:

- 3 cups fresh chopped romaine
- ½ cup cherry tomatoes, halved
- ½ cup chopped cucumber, seedless
- ¼ cup diced red onion
- 1 lemon, juiced
- 2 (5-ounce) cans tuna in water

Instructions:

1. Combine the romaine lettuce, tomatoes, cucumber, and red onion in a large salad bowl.
2. Toss with lemon juice then season with salt and pepper.
3. Divide the salad among two plates.
4. Drain and flake the tuna then divide it between the two salads to serve.

Nutrition: 205 calories, 4.5g fat, 34.5g protein, 5g carbs, 1g fiber, 4g net carbs

Pumpkin Ginger Soup

Servings: 3

Ingredients:

- 1 cup fresh pumpkin
- 1 tablespoon olive oil
- ½ small yellow onion, chopped
- 1 clove minced garlic
- 1 tablespoon grated ginger
- 2 cups chicken broth

Instructions:

1. Bring a pot of salted water to boil then add the fresh pumpkin.
2. Boil until the pumpkin is soften then drain and mash it well.
3. Heat the oil in a saucepan over medium heat.
4. Add the onion, garlic, and ginger then cook for 3 minutes, stirring.
5. Add the pumpkin then cook for 2 minutes.
6. Stir in the chicken broth then bring to a boil.
7. Reduce heat and simmer for 20 minutes then remove from heat.
8. Puree the soup using an immersion blender then adjust seasoning to taste.

Nutrition: 60 calories, 9g fat, 7g protein, 15g carbs, 5g fiber, 10g net carbs

Bacon Arugula Salad with Mushrooms

Servings: 2

Ingredients:

- 3 slices bacon
- 1 cup sliced mushrooms
- 1 small shallot, sliced thin

- 4 cups fresh baby arugula

Instructions:

1. Cook the bacon in a skillet until crisp then remove to paper towels to drain.
2. Spoon all but 1 tablespoon of bacon fat out of the skillet and reheat it.
3. Add the mushrooms and shallots then sauté until they are tender, about 4 to 6 minutes.
4. Divide the arugula between two salad bowls.
5. Top with the mushrooms and crumble the bacon over the salads.
6. Serve with olive oil and vinegar.

Nutrition: 105 calories, 6.5g fat, 8g protein, 4.5g carbs, 1g fiber, 3.5g net carbs

Broccoli Cheddar Soup

Servings: 4

Ingredients:

- 1 tablespoon butter
- ½ small white onion, diced
- 1 cup chopped broccoli
- 2 cups chicken broth
- ¼ cup heavy cream
- 1 cup shredded cheddar cheese

Instructions:

1. Sauté the onion in butter in a saucepan over medium heat until the onions are translucent.
2. Stir in the broccoli and chicken broth then bring to a boil.
3. Reduce heat and simmer until the broccoli is tender, about 10 to 12 minutes.
4. Stir in the cream then season with salt and pepper.

5. Remove from heat then stir in the cheddar cheese. Serve hot.

Nutrition: 200 calories, 16g fat, 10.5g protein, 3.5g carbs, 1g fiber, 2.5g net carbs

Tuna Salad on Lettuce

Servings: 3

Ingredients:

- 1 (5-ounce) can tuna in water, drained
- 1 medium stalk celery, diced
- ½ cup mayonnaise
- 1 tablespoon lemon juice
- 1 teaspoon Dijon mustard
- 3 cups chopped romaine lettuce

Instructions:

1. Flake the tuna into a bowl then add the celery.
2. Stir in the mayonnaise, lemon juice, and mustard then season with salt and pepper.
3. Serve the tuna salad over chopped lettuce.

Nutrition: 315 calories, 28g fat, 11.5g protein, 2.5g carbs, 1g fiber, 1.5g net carbs

Buffalo Chicken Soup

Servings: 4

Ingredients:

- 2 tablespoons butter
- ½ small yellow onion, chopped
- 2 cups half-n-half
- 1 cup chopped chicken breast
- 2 tablespoons hot sauce
- 1 cup shredded cheddar cheese

Instructions:

1. Heat the butter in a saucepan on medium-high heat.
2. Add the onion and sauté until tender then stir in the flour.
3. Cook for another 2 minutes then add the half-and-half.
4. Stir in the chicken, hot sauce, and cheddar cheese then season with salt and pepper.
5. Reduce heat and simmer on medium-low until the cheese is melted, about 10 minutes.

Nutrition: 355 calories, 30g fat, 16g protein, 6.5g carbs. 0.5g fiber, 6g net carbs

Spinach Salad with Bacon Dressing

Servings: 2

Ingredients:

- 4 cups fresh baby spinach
- 4 slices bacon
- 1 ½ tablespoons apple cider vinegar
- 2 teaspoons honey
- 2 teaspoon Dijon mustard
- 2 hard-boiled eggs, sliced

Instructions:

1. Divide the spinach between two salad plates.
2. Cook the bacon in a small skillet over medium-high heat until crisp.
3. Remove the bacon to paper towels to drain then crumble.
4. Spoon all but 2 tablespoons of bacon grease out of the skillet then reheat it.
5. Whisk in the vinegar, honey, and mustard then season with salt and pepper.
6. Cook until warmed then drizzle over the salads.
7. Top each salad with sliced egg to serve.

Nutrition: 210 calories, 13g fat, 14.5g protein, 9g carbs, 1.5g fiber, 7.5g net carbs

Cucumber Avocado Soup

Servings: 3

Ingredients:

- 1 medium seedless cucumber, peeled and chopped
- 1 small avocado, chopped
- ¼ cup fresh cilantro
- 2 tablespoons apple cider vinegar
- 1 clove minced garlic
- ¾ cup water

Instructions:

1. Combine the cucumber, avocado, cilantro, vinegar, and garlic in a blender and blend until smooth and well combined.
2. Add up to 1 cup of water, a little at a time, until thinned to the desired texture.
3. Season with salt and pepper then chill until ready to serve.

Nutrition: 150 calories, 13g fat, 2g protein, 7.5g carbs, 5g fiber, 2.5g net carbs

Easy Egg Salad on Lettuce

Servings: 4

Ingredients:

- 6 large eggs
- 1 medium avocado, chopped
- 1/3 cup mayonnaise
- 1 teaspoon Dijon mustard
- 1 teaspoon lemon juice
- 3 cups fresh chopped romaine

Instructions:

1. Hard-boil the eggs to your liking then rinse in cold water and peel.
2. Chop the eggs into a bowl then season with salt and pepper.
3. Mash the avocado then stir it into the egg with the mayonnaise, mustard, and lemon juice.
4. Serve the egg salad chilled on chopped romaine lettuce.

Nutrition: 350 calories, 32g fat, 10.5g protein, 5g carbs, 3.5g fiber, 1.5g net carbs

Mexican Chicken Soup

Servings: 2

Ingredients:

- ½ pound boneless chicken thighs
- ½ cup diced tomatoes
- ½ small yellow onion, chopped
- 2 cloves minced garlic
- 1 cup chicken broth
- ½ cup shredded cheddar cheese

Instructions:

1. Combine the chicken, tomatoes, onion, and garlic in a slow cooker.
2. Pour in the chicken broth then season with salt and pepper.
3. Cover and cook on high heat for 2 to 3 hours then shred the chicken.
4. Stir in the cheddar cheese and cook for another 20 minutes.
5. Serve hot topped with sour cream and diced avocado.

Nutrition: 400 calories, 27g fat, 30g protein, 5g carbs, 1g fiber, 4g net carbs

Greek-Style Salad with Feta

Servings: 2

Ingredients:

- 2 tablespoons olive oil
- 1 tablespoon red wine vinegar
- 3 cups chopped romaine lettuce
- ½ cup diced seedless cucumber, peeled
- ½ cup kalamata olives, sliced
- 1.5 ounces feta cheese, crumbled

Instructions:

1. Whisk together the olive oil and red wine vinegar in a salad bowl.
2. Toss in the lettuce, cucumber, and olives.
3. Divide the salad between two salad bowls and top with feta to serve.

Nutrition: 230 calories, 22g fat, 4g protein, 6.5g carbs, 2g fiber, 4.5g net carb

Creamy Tomato Bisque

Servings: 3

Ingredients:

- 1 teaspoon olive oil
- ½ small yellow onion, chopped
- 2 cloves minced garlic
- 2 cups chicken broth
- 1 (14-ounce) can crushed tomatoes
- ¼ cup heavy cream

Instructions:

1. Heat the oil in a saucepan over medium heat.
2. Add the onion and garlic then sauté until the onion is soft, about 6 minutes.
3. Stir in the chicken broth and tomatoes then bring to a simmer.
4. Cook for 30 minutes then remove from heat and blend smooth.
5. Stir in the heavy cream and season with salt and pepper.

Nutrition: 135 calories, 6g fat, 7g protein, 13g carbs, 4.5g fiber, 8.5g net carbs

Chopped Cobb Salad with Avocado

Servings: 2

Ingredients:

- 4 cups chopped romaine lettuce
- ½ medium avocado, diced
- 1 cup chopped chicken breast
- ½ cup cherry tomatoes
- 1 ounce blue cheese crumbles
- 2 hard-boiled eggs

Instructions:

1. Divide the romaine lettuce between two salad bowls.
2. Finely dice the avocado, chicken, and tomatoes.
3. Arrange the chopped ingredients on top of the two salads.
4. Sprinkle with blue cheese and top each salad with a hardboiled egg.
5. Serve with olive oil and vinegar.

Nutrition: 300 calories, 20g fat, 20.5g protein, 10.5g carbs, 4.5g fiber, 6g net carbs

Broccoli Salmon Casserole

Servings: 4

Ingredients:

- 1 tablespoon butter
- 1 pound fresh chopped broccoli
- 3 (6-ounce) cans Alaskan salmon, drained
- 1 cup heavy cream
- 1 tablespoon Dijon mustard
- 1 cup shredded cheddar cheese

Instructions:

1. Preheat the oven to 400°F and lightly grease an 8x8-inch glass dish.
2. Heat the butter in a medium skillet over medium heat then add the broccoli.
3. Sauté for 6 to 7 minutes until tender then spread in the baking dish.
4. Flake the salmon over the broccoli and season with salt and pepper.
5. Whisk the cream with the mustard and pour into the baking dish.
6. Sprinkle with cheddar cheese then bake for 20 minutes until hot and bubbling.

Nutrition: 495 calories, 33g fat, 41g protein, 9g carbs, 3g fiber, 6g net carbs

Steak and Pepper Kebabs

Servings: 3

Ingredients:

- 12 ounces sirloin steak
- 2 tablespoons olive oil
- 1 ½ tablespoons balsamic vinegar
- 1 teaspoon Dijon mustard
- Salt and pepper
- 2 small red peppers, cored and cut into chunks

Instructions:

1. Cut the beef into cubes and toss with olive oil, balsamic vinegar, and mustard.
2. Slice the beef onto metal skewers with the peppers.
3. Season the kebabs with salt and pepper.
4. Preheat the grill to high heat and grease the grates with oil.
5. Place the kebabs on the grill and cook for 2 to 3 minutes on each side until the steak is done to your liking.

Nutrition: 320 calories, 16.5g fat, 35g protein, 6g carbs, 1g fiber, 5g net carbs

Smothered Pork Chops

Servings: 3

Ingredients:

- 1 tablespoon olive oil
- 2 cups sliced mushrooms
- ½ small yellow onion, sliced thin
- 12 ounces boneless pork loin chops
- ¼ cup chicken broth
- ½ cup heavy cream

Instructions:

1. Heat the oil in a large skillet on medium-high heat.
2. Add the mushrooms and onions then sauté until browned, about 5 minutes.
3. Season the pork with salt and pepper then add to the skillet.
4. Cook for 3 minutes then turn the pork chops over and lower the heat to medium.
5. Cook for 8 to 10 minutes until the pork is cooked through then remove to a cutting board to rest.
6. Pour the broth into the skillet and simmer, scraping up the browned bits, until the liquid cooks off.
7. Stir in the cream and simmer until hot then spoon over the pork to serve.

Nutrition: 290 calories, 16g fat, 32g protein, 3.5g carbs, 1g fiber, 2.5g net carbs

Herb-Roasted Chicken

Servings: 4

Ingredients:

- 8 bone-in chicken thighs
- 1 tablespoon olive oil
- 2 cups chopped cauliflower
- 1 ½ cups sliced green beans
- ¼ cup chicken broth
- 1 tablespoon dried herbs (your choice)

Instructions:

1. Preheat the oven to 450°F and lightly grease a glass baking dish.
2. Heat the oil in a large skillet over medium-high heat.
3. Season the chicken with salt and pepper then add to the skillet.
4. Cook skin-side down for 3 to 4 minutes until the skin is browned then flip and cook for another 2 minutes on the other side.
5. Toss the veggies with the chicken broth and spread in the baking dish.
6. Place the chicken skin-side down on top of the veggies and roast 30 minutes.
7. Turn the chicken skin-side up and sprinkle with herbs.
8. Roast for another 25 to 30 minutes until cooked through then serve with the roasted veggies.

Nutrition: 420 calories, 29g fat, 32g protein, 6g carbs, 3g fiber, 3g net carbs

Grilled Pesto Salmon

Servings: 2

Ingredients:

- 2 (6-ounce) boneless salmon fillets
- Salt and pepper
- 16 spears asparagus
- 1 tablespoon olive oil
- 2 tablespoons pesto
- Lemon wedges

Instructions:

1. Preheat a grill pan to high heat and grease with cooking spray.
2. Season the salmon with salt and pepper then place it on the grill.
3. Toss the asparagus with the oil and place on the grill – cook until tender, turning occasionally as needed.
4. Cook the salmon for 4 to 5 minutes on each side until cooked to your liking.
5. Spread the pesto over the salmon and serve with lemon wedges.

Nutrition: 390 calories, 24g fat, 38.5g protein, 8.5g carbs, 4.5g fiber, 4g net carbs

Cheese-Stuffed Burgers

Servings: 3

Ingredients:

- 12 ounces ground beef (80% lean)
- 3 tablespoons almond flour
- 1 large egg
- ¾ cups shredded cheddar cheese
- 1 tablespoon olive oil
- 1 head Boston lettuce, leaves separated

Instructions:

1. Stir together the ground beef, almond flour, egg, and cheese in a bowl.
2. Season with salt and pepper then divide into 3 patties.
3. Heat the oil in a large skillet on medium-high heat then add the burgers.
4. Cook for 5 minutes then flip the burgers and cook to your liking.
5. Serve the burgers with your favorite keto burger toppings on lettuce leaves.

Nutrition: 400 calories, 23g fat, 44g protein, 2g carbs, 1g fiber, 1g net carbs

Rosemary Pork Tenderloin

Servings: 3

Ingredients:

- 1 ¼ pounds boneless pork tenderloin
- 1 tablespoon butter
- 1 tablespoon fresh chopped rosemary
- Salt and pepper
- 1 tablespoon olive oil
- 2 cups chopped broccoli

Instructions:

1. Rub the pork tenderloin with butter then season with rosemary, salt, and pepper.
2. Heat the oil in a large skillet over medium-high heat.
3. Place the pork in the hot skillet and cook for 2 to 3 minutes on each side to sear.
4. Add the broccoli to the skillet around the pork.
5. Reduce heat and cook on low, covered, for 8 to 10 minutes until the pork reaches an internal temperature of 145°F.

Nutrition: 300 calories, 14g fat, 37g protein, 6.5g carbs, 2g fiber, 4.5g net carbs

Seared Lamb Chops

Servings: 2

Ingredients:

- 4 bone-in lamb chops
- Salt and pepper
- 1 tablespoon olive oil
- 1 tablespoon butter
- 1 ½ cups sliced green beans

Instructions:

1. Season the lamb with salt and pepper.
2. Heat the oil in a large skillet over medium-high heat.
3. Add the lamb chops to the skillet and cook for 2 minutes until seared.
4. Turn the lamb chops and cook for 2 to 3 minutes on the other side until seared.
5. Remove the lamb chops to a cutting board to rest and reheat the skillet.
6. Melt the butter then add the green beans.
7. Sauté the green beans until tender then serve with the lamb chops.

Nutrition: 360 calories, 22g fat, 36g protein, 6g carbs, 3g fiber, 3g net carbs

Almond-Crusted Haddock

Servings: 4

Ingredients:

- 4 (6-ounce) boneless haddock fillets
- Salt and pepper
- ¼ cup almond flour
- 3 tablespoons chopped almonds
- ½ teaspoon garlic powder
- 1 large egg

Instructions:

1. Preheat the oven to 350°F and line a baking sheet with parchment.
2. Season the fish with salt and pepper.
3. Combine the almond flour, chopped almonds, and garlic powder in a shallow dish.
4. Whisk the egg then dip the fish fillets in the egg and dredge in the almond mixture.
5. Place the fillets on the baking sheet and bake for 12 to 15 minutes until the flesh flakes easily with a fork.
6. Serve the almond-crusted haddock with lemon wedges.

Nutrition: 230 calories, 8g fat, 35.5g protein, 2.5g carbs, 1g fiber, 1.5g net carbs

Curry Chicken and Broccoli

Servings: 4

Ingredients:

- ½ tablespoon curry powder
- 1 teaspoon garlic powder
- 1 teaspoon ground cumin
- 1 ½ pounds boneless chicken thighs
- 2 tablespoons olive oil
- 3 cups fresh chopped broccoli

Instructions:

1. Preheat the oven to 425°F and line a baking sheet with parchment.
2. Whisk together the curry powder, garlic powder, and cumin in a small bowl.
3. Toss the chicken thighs to coat with oil then sprinkle with the spice mixture and toss to coat it.
4. Place the chicken thighs on the baking sheet and add the broccoli around it.
5. Bake for 45 to 50 minutes until the chicken is done and the broccoli tender.

Nutrition: 450 calories, 33g fat, 32g protein, 6g carbs, 2.5g fiber, 3.5g net carbs

Pepper Grilled Steak

Servings: 4

Ingredients:

- 1 medium head cauliflower, chopped
- 2 tablespoons olive oil
- 1 pound ribeye steak
- Fresh ground pepper

Instructions:

1. Preheat the oven to 400°F and line a baking sheet with foil.
2. Toss the cauliflower with the oil and spread it on the baking sheet.
3. Season with salt and pepper, bake for 25 minutes while you prepare the steak.
4. Generously pepper the steak and season it with salt.
5. Grease an oven-proof skillet with cooking spray and heat it over high heat.
6. Add the steak and cook for 2 minutes then turn the steak over.
7. Transfer the steak to the oven and cook for 5 minutes or until done to your liking.
8. Serve the steak sliced with the roasted cauliflower.

Nutrition: 475 calories, 40g fat, 22g protein, 7.5g carbs, 3.5g fiber, 4g net carbs

Sesame Chicken Wings

Servings: 4

Ingredients:

- 3 tablespoons soy sauce
- 1 ½ tablespoons sesame oil
- 2 teaspoon balsamic vinegar
- 2 cloves minced garlic
- 16 chicken wing pieces
- 1 tablespoon sesame seeds

Instructions:

1. Whisk together the soy sauce, sesame oil, balsamic vinegar, and garlic.
2. Place the chicken wings in a zippered freezer bag and pour in the sauce.
3. Shake until well coated then marinate in the fridge for 2 hours.
4. Preheat the oven to 400°F and line a baking sheet with foil.
5. Remove the wings from the bag and shake off the extra sauce.
6. Place the wings on the baking sheet and bake for 35 minutes.
7. Sprinkle with sesame seeds and serve hot.

Nutrition: 460 calories, 33g fat, 38g protein, 2g carbs, 0.5g fiber, 1.5g net carbs

Cheesy Sausage Casserole

Servings: 6

Ingredients:

- 1 pound mild Italian ground sausage
- 8 ounces sliced mushrooms
- ½ small yellow onion, chopped
- 1 cup shredded cheddar jack cheese
- 8 large eggs
- ½ cup heavy cream

Instructions:

1. Preheat the oven to 375°F and grease a medium baking dish.
2. Cook the sausage in a skillet over medium-high heat until browned.
3. Stir in the mushrooms and onions and sauté until tender, about 6 to 8 minutes.
4. Spread the mixture in the baking dish and sprinkle with cheese.
5. Whisk together the eggs and heavy cream then pour over the ingredients.
6. Bake for 35 minutes until hot and bubbling.

Nutrition: 440 calories, 33g fat, 27g protein, 4.5g carbs, 1g fiber, 3.5g net carbs

Easy Shrimp Curry

Servings: 4

Ingredients:

- 2 cups chopped cauliflower
- 1 teaspoon olive oil
- 1 cup canned coconut milk
- 1 tablespoon minced garlic
- 1 teaspoon garam masala
- 1 pound large uncooked shrimp, peeled and deveined

Instructions:

1. Place the cauliflower in a food processor and pulse until it forms rice-like grains.
2. Heat the oil in a large skillet over medium heat.
3. Add the cauliflower and sauté for 6 to 8 minutes until tender.
4. Stir in the coconut milk, garlic, and garam masala then bring to a simmer.
5. Add the shrimp and simmer until they are just cooked through. Serve hot.

Nutrition: 225 calories, 16g fat, 17g protein, 6.5g carbs, 2.5g fiber, 4g net carbs

Turkey-Stuffed Peppers

Servings: 3

Ingredients:

- 1 small head cauliflower, chopped
- 1 teaspoon olive oil
- 12 ounces mild Italian ground sausage
- 1 teaspoon dried oregano
- 3 small bell peppers
- ½ cup shredded mozzarella cheese

Instructions:

1. Preheat the oven to 350°F.
2. Place the cauliflower in a food processor and pulse until it forms rice-like grains.
3. Heat the oil in a large skillet over medium heat.
4. Add the cauliflower and sauté for 6 to 8 minutes until tender.
5. Spoon the cauliflower rice into a bowl and reheat the skillet with the sausage.
6. Cook until the sausage is browned then stir the cauliflower back in.
7. Add the oregano then season with salt and pepper.
8. Slice the tops off the peppers and spoon the meat mixture into them then sprinkle with cheese.
9. Place the peppers in a dish and bake for 30 minutes, covered.
10. Uncover and bake for another 15 minutes until the peppers are tender.

Nutrition: 430 calories, 29g fat, 24g protein, 15g carbs, 4g fiber, 11g net carbs

Almond Green Smoothie

Servings: 1

Ingredients:

- 1 cup unsweetened almond milk
- ½ cup full-fat Greek yogurt, plain
- 1 cup fresh baby spinach
- 1 small stalk celery, sliced
- ½ tablespoon almond butter
- Liquid stevia, to taste

Instructions:

1. Combine all of the ingredients in a blender.
2. Pulse several times then blend until smooth.
3. Sweeten to taste with liquid stevia then blend smooth.
4. Pour into a large glass and enjoy immediately.

Nutrition: 220 calories, 14g fat, 14g protein, 10.5g carbs, 3g fiber, 7.5g net carbs

Red Velvet Cake Smoothie

Servings: 1

Ingredients:

- 1 cup unsweetened almond milk
- ½ cup canned coconut milk
- ½ small beet, peeled and diced
- 1 teaspoon unsweetened cocoa powder
- ½ teaspoon vanilla extract

Instructions:

1. Combine all of the ingredients in a blender.
2. Pulse several times then blend until smooth.
3. Sweeten to taste with liquid stevia then blend smooth.
4. Pour into a large glass and enjoy immediately.

Nutrition: 295 calories, 28g fat, 4.5g protein, 11.5g carbs, 2.5g fiber, 9g net carbs

Avocado Spinach Smoothie

Servings: 1

Ingredients:

- 1 cup fresh baby spinach
- ½ cup diced avocado
- 1 cup unsweetened almond milk
- 4 to 5 ice cubes
- 1 tablespoon lemon juice
- Liquid stevia, to taste

Instructions:

1. Combine all of the ingredients in a blender.
2. Pulse several times then blend until smooth.
3. Sweeten to taste with liquid stevia then blend smooth.
4. Pour into a large glass and enjoy immediately.

Nutrition: 200 calories, 18g fat, 3.5g protein, 9.5g carbs, 6.5g fiber, 3g net carbs

Raspberry Coconut Smoothie

Servings: 1

Ingredients:

- 1 cup unsweetened almond milk
- ¼ cup canned coconut milk
- 4 fresh raspberries
- 4 to 5 ice cubes
- ½ teaspoon vanilla extract
- Liquid stevia, to taste

Instructions:

1. Combine all of the ingredients in a blender.
2. Pulse several times then blend until smooth.
3. Sweeten to taste with liquid stevia then blend smooth.
4. Pour into a large glass and enjoy immediately.

Nutrition: 220 calories, 18.5g fat, 3.5g protein, 14g carbs, 7g fiber, 7g net carbs

Almond Butter Protein Shake

Servings: 1

Ingredients:

- 1 cup unsweetened almond milk
- ¼ cup canned coconut milk
- 1 scoop vanilla whey protein powder
- ½ tablespoon almond butter
- Pinch ground cinnamon
- Liquid stevia, to taste

Instructions:

1. Combine all of the ingredients in a blender.
2. Pulse several times then blend until smooth.
3. Sweeten to taste with liquid stevia then blend smooth.
4. Pour into a large glass and enjoy immediately.

Nutrition: 345 calories, 24g fat, 26g protein, 9g carbs, 3.5g fiber, 5.5g net carbs

Cocoa Avocado Smoothie

Servings: 1

Ingredients:

- 1 cup unsweetened almond milk
- ½ cup chopped avocado
- 4 to 5 ice cubes
- 1 scoop chocolate whey protein powder
- Liquid stevia, to taste

Instructions:

1. Combine all of the ingredients in a blender.
2. Pulse several times then blend until smooth.
3. Sweeten to taste with liquid stevia then blend smooth.
4. Pour into a large glass and enjoy immediately.

Nutrition: 245 calories, 18.5g fat, 12.5g protein, 10g carbs, 6g fiber, 4g net carbs

Blueberry and Beet Smoothie

Servings: 1

Ingredients:

- 1 cup unsweetened almond milk
- ¼ cup canned coconut milk
- 1 tablespoon blueberries
- ½ small beet, peeled and chopped
- Liquid stevia, to taste

Instructions:

1. Combine all of the ingredients in a blender.
2. Pulse several times then blend until smooth.
3. Sweeten to taste with liquid stevia then blend smooth.
4. Pour into a large glass and enjoy immediately.

Nutrition: 205 calories, 18g fat, 3.5g protein, 11.5g carbs, 3.5g fiber, 8g net carbs

Choco-Macadamia Smoothie

Servings: 1

Ingredients:

- 1 cup unsweetened almond milk
- ¼ cup canned coconut milk
- 4 macadamia nuts, chopped
- 1 tablespoon unsweetened shredded coconut
- Pinch ground ginger
- Liquid stevia, to taste

Instructions:

1. Combine all of the ingredients in a blender.
2. Pulse several times then blend until smooth.

3. Sweeten to taste with liquid stevia then blend smooth.
4. Pour into a large glass and enjoy immediately.

Nutrition: 360 calories, 35g fat, 4g protein, 11g carbs, 5g fiber, 6g net carbs

Lemon Lime Smoothie

Servings: 1

Ingredients:

- 1 cup fresh chopped spinach
- ½ cup diced avocado
- 1 cup water
- 4 to 5 ice cubes
- 1 scoop vanilla whey protein powder
- 2 tablespoons fresh lemon juice
- 1 tablespoon fresh lime juice

Instructions:

1. Combine all of the ingredients in a blender.
2. Pulse several times then blend until smooth.
3. Sweeten to taste with liquid stevia then blend smooth.
4. Pour into a large glass and enjoy immediately.

Nutrition: 280 calories, 16.5g fat, 24.5g protein, 10g carbs, 5.5g fiber, 4.5g net carbs

Strawberry Cheesecake Smoothie

Servings: 1

Ingredients:

- 1 cup unsweetened almond milk
- 1 scoop vanilla whey protein powder
- 2 tablespoons cream cheese, softened
- ¼ cup fresh raspberries
- ½ teaspoon vanilla extract
- Liquid stevia, to taste

Instructions:

1. Combine all of the ingredients in a blender.
2. Pulse several times then blend until smooth.
3. Sweeten to taste with liquid stevia then blend smooth.
4. Pour into a large glass and enjoy immediately.

Nutrition: 325 calories, 21g fat, 26.5g protein, 9g carbs, 3g fiber, 6g net carbs

Pumpkin Pie Protein Shake

Servings: 1

Ingredients:

- 1 cup unsweetened almond milk
- ¼ cup canned coconut milk
- 1 scoop vanilla whey protein powder
- 2 tablespoons pumpkin puree
- ¼ teaspoon pumpkin pie spice
- Liquid stevia, to taste

Instructions:

1. Combine all of the ingredients in a blender.
2. Pulse several times then blend until smooth.
3. Sweeten to taste with liquid stevia then blend smooth.
4. Pour into a large glass and enjoy immediately.

Nutrition: 305 calories, 20g fat, 25g protein, 10g carbs, 3.5g fiber, 6.5g net carbs

Vanilla Chai Smoothie

Servings: 1

Ingredients:

- 1 cup unsweetened almond milk
- 1/3 cup canned coconut milk
- 4 to 5 ice cubes
- 1 teaspoon vanilla extract
- ¼ teaspoon ground cinnamon
- ¼ teaspoon ground ginger
- Pinch cloves

Instructions:

1. Combine all of the ingredients in a blender.
2. Pulse several times then blend until smooth.
3. Sweeten to taste with liquid stevia then blend smooth.
4. Pour into a large glass and enjoy immediately.

Nutrition: 265 calories, 25g fat, 3g protein, 8.5g carbs, 3.5g fiber, 5g net carbs

Lemon Avocado Smoothie

Servings: 1

Ingredients:

- 1 cup fresh baby spinach
- 1/2 cup chopped avocado
- 1 small stalk celery, chopped
- 1 cup cold water
- 4 to 5 ice cubes
- 1 tablespoon lemon juice

Instructions:

1. Combine all of the ingredients in a blender.
2. Pulse several times then blend until smooth.
3. Sweeten to taste with liquid stevia then blend smooth.
4. Pour into a large glass and enjoy immediately.

Nutrition: 160 calories, 14.5g fat, 2.5g protein, 8g carbs, 6g fiber, 2g net carbs

Cucumber Melon Smoothie

Servings: 1

Ingredients:

- 1 cup unsweetened almond milk
- ½ cup seedless cucumber, peeled and chopped
- ¼ cup chopped honeydew melon
- ¼ cup canned coconut milk
- 4 to 5 ice cubes
- 1 tablespoon lemon juice
- Liquid stevia, to taste

Instructions:

1. Combine all of the ingredients in a blender.
2. Pulse several times then blend until smooth.
3. Sweeten to taste with liquid stevia then blend smooth.
4. Pour into a large glass and enjoy immediately.

Nutrition: 205 calories, 18g fat, 3g protein, 11g carbs, 3g fiber, 8g net carbs

Cocoa Almond Smoothie

Servings: 1

Ingredients:

- 1 cup unsweetened almond milk
- ¼ cup canned coconut milk
- 1 scoop vanilla whey protein powder
- 1 tablespoon unsweetened cocoa powder
- Liquid stevia, to taste

Instructions:

1. Combine all of the ingredients in a blender.
2. Pulse several times then blend until smooth.
3. Sweeten to taste with liquid stevia then blend smooth.
4. Pour into a large glass and enjoy immediately.

Nutrition: 305 calories, 20.5g fat, 25.5g protein, 10g carbs, 4g fiber, 6g net carbs

Chocolate Almond Fat Bombs

Servings: 8

Ingredients:

- ½ cup coconut oil
- ½ cup almond butter
- ¼ cup cocoa powder
- 2 tablespoons coconut flour
- Liquid stevia, to taste
- 8 whole almonds

Instructions:

1. Combine the coconut oil and almond butter in a small saucepan over low heat until melted then whisk smooth.
2. Whisk in the cocoa powder along with the coconut flour.
3. Stir smooth then sweeten with liquid stevia to taste and remove from heat.
4. When the mixture hardens slightly, divide it into 8 pieces and roll into balls.
5. Top each ball with an almond then chill until firm.

Nutrition: 150 calories, 15.5g fat, 1.5g protein, 4g carbs, 2.5g fiber, 1.5g net carbs

Cashew Butter Fat Bombs

Servings: 8

Ingredients:

- ½ cup coconut oil
- ½ cup cashew butter
- ¼ cup unsweetened cocoa powder
- 2 tablespoons coconut flour
- Liquid stevia
- 8 whole cashews

Instructions:

1. Combine the coconut oil and cashew butter in a small saucepan over low heat until melted then whisk smooth.
2. Whisk in the cocoa powder along with the coconut flour.
3. Stir smooth then sweeten with liquid stevia to taste and remove from heat.
4. When the mixture hardens slightly, divide it into 8 pieces and roll into balls.
5. Top each ball with a cashew then chill until firm.

Nutrition: 240 calories, 23g fat, 4g protein, 8.5g carbs, 2.5g fiber, 6g net carbs

Macadamia Nut Fat Bombs

Servings: 8

Ingredients:

- ½ cup coconut oil
- ½ cup almond butter
- ¼ cup unsweetened cocoa powder
- 2 tablespoons coconut flour
- Liquid stevia
- 8 macadamia nuts

Instructions:

1. Combine the coconut oil and almond butter in a small saucepan over low heat until melted then whisk smooth.
2. Whisk in the cocoa powder along with the coconut flour.
3. Stir smooth then sweeten with liquid stevia to taste and remove from heat.
4. When the mixture hardens slightly, divide it into 8 pieces and roll into balls.
5. Top each ball with a macadamia nut then chill until firm.

Nutrition: 165 calories, 17g fat, 1.5g protein, 4g carbs, 2.5g fiber, 1.5g net carbs

Chocolate Sunflower Fat Bombs

Servings: 8

Ingredients:

- ½ cup coconut oil
- ½ cup sunflower seed butter
- ¼ cup unsweetened cocoa powder, divided
- 2 tablespoons coconut flour
- Liquid stevia, to taste

Instructions:

1. Combine the coconut oil and sunflower seed butter in a small saucepan over low heat until melted then whisk smooth.
2. Whisk in half the cocoa powder along with the coconut flour.
3. Stir smooth then sweeten with liquid stevia to taste and remove from heat.
4. When the mixture hardens slightly, divide it into 8 pieces and roll into balls.
5. Roll each ball in the remaining cocoa powder then chill until firm.

Nutrition: 230 calories, 22g fat, 4g protein, 8g carbs, 2g fiber, 6g net carbs

Sesame Seed Fat Bombs

Servings:

Ingredients:

- ½ cup coconut oil
- ½ cup almond butter
- ¼ cup unsweetened cocoa powder
- 2 tablespoons almond flour
- Liquid stevia
- ¼ cup toasted sesame seeds

Instructions:

1. Combine the coconut oil and almond butter in a small saucepan over low heat until melted then whisk smooth.
2. Whisk in the cocoa powder along with the almond flour.
3. Stir smooth then sweeten with liquid stevia to taste and remove from heat.
4. When the mixture hardens slightly, divide it into 8 pieces and roll into balls.
5. Roll each ball in the sesame seeds then chill until firm.

Nutrition: 165 calories, 17.5g fat, 2g protein, 3g carbs, 1.5g fiber, 1.5g net carbs

Classic Deviled Eggs

Servings: 12

Ingredients:

- 12 large eggs
- ½ cup mayonnaise
- 1 tablespoon Dijon mustard
- 2 teaspoons fresh lemon juice
- Salt to taste
- Paprika

Instructions:

1. Hard-boil the eggs then rinse in cool water and peel them.
2. Cut the eggs in half lengthwise and scoop the yolks into a bowl.
3. Mash the yolks with the mayonnaise, mustard, lemon juice, and salt.
4. Spoon or pipe the filling back into the eggs and sprinkle with paprika to serve.

Nutrition: 130 calories, 12g fat, 6.5g protein, 0.5g carbs, 0g fiber, 0.5g net carbs

Cinnamon Spiced Almonds

Servings: 4

Ingredients:

- 1 cup almonds, whole
- 1 tablespoon olive oil
- 1 teaspoon ground cinnamon
- Pinch salt

Instructions:

1. Preheat the oven to 300°F and line a baking sheet with foil.
2. Toss the almonds with the olive oil, cinnamon, and salt.
3. Spread the almonds on the baking sheet and bake for 25 minutes.
4. Cool completely then store in an airtight container.

Nutrition: 170 calories, 15.5g fat, 5g protein, 5.5g carbs, 3.5g fiber, 2g net carbs

Baked Sesame Chia Crackers

Servings: 4

Ingredients:

- ¾ cup almond flour
- ¼ cup sesame seeds
- 1 tablespoon chia seeds
- ¼ teaspoon salt
- 2 teaspoons coconut oil, melted
- 1 large egg white

Instructions:

1. Preheat the oven to 350°F and line a baking sheet with parchment.
2. Whisk together the almond flour, sesame seeds, chia seeds, and salt.
3. Add the coconut oil and egg, stirring it into a soft dough.
4. Roll the dough out to 1/8-inch thick then cut it into squares.
5. Arrange the squares on the baking sheet and bake for 10 to 12 minutes until browned.

Nutrition: 200 calories, 18g fat, 7.5g protein, 7g carbs, 4g fiber, 3g net carbs

Coconut Chia Pudding

Servings: 3

Ingredients:

- 1 ¼ cup canned coconut milk
- 1 teaspoon vanilla extract
- ¼ teaspoon coconut extract
- Pinch salt
- Liquid stevia, to taste
- ¼ cup chia seeds

Instructions:

1. Whisk together the coconut milk, extracts, and salt in a bowl.
2. Sweeten with liquid stevia to taste then whisk in the chia seeds.
3. Cover and chill overnight then spoon into bowls to serve.

Nutrition: 315 calories, 30g fat, 6.5g protein, 12.5g carbs, 9g fiber, 3.5g net carbs

Baked Kale Chips

Servings: 4

Ingredients:

- 1 bunch fresh kale
- 1 tablespoon olive oil
- Salt and pepper

Instructions:

1. Preheat the oven to 350°F and line a baking sheet with foil.
2. Cut the kale into 2-inch pieces, removing the tough stems.
3. Toss with olive oil, salt, and pepper then spread on the baking sheet.
4. Bake for 10 to 12 minutes until crisp.

Nutrition: 50 calories, 3.5g fat, 1.5g protein, 4.5g carbs, 0.5g fiber, 4g net carbs

Conclusion

Well, there you have it! The ketogenic diet in all its glory.

By now, you should feel like an expert on the ketogenic diet and, to a certain degree, you are! You have learned everything you need to know to get started with the diet and to use it as a tool to lose weight and improve your health.

The beauty of the keto diet is that you don't have to scrimp and starve – you can enjoy healthy and satisfying meals without worrying about consuming too much fat. There is no such thing as too much fat on the ketogenic diet! In fact, the more fat you consume, the more energy your body will have to burn!

Though it may take some time for you to get used to the dietary changes required to maintain a ketogenic diet, you have all the tools you need to get started. In this book, you've received an overview of the diet and its benefits as well as three weekly meal plans complete with shopping lists. What could be easier than that?

So, if you're ready to kiss your fat goodbye and give the ketogenic diet a try, don't wait a moment longer. Get going!

Best of luck to you!

Printed in Great Britain
by Amazon